RUSSIAN ART COLORING BOOK

---

*Russian Masterpieces
from Shishkin to Vasnetsov*

NICOLAS SMOLNIY

"The world is but a canvas to our imagination."
—Henry David Thoreau

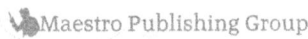Maestro Publishing Group

Pubished by Maestro Publishing Group

Printed in the United States of America
ISBN: 978-1619494824

CONTENTS

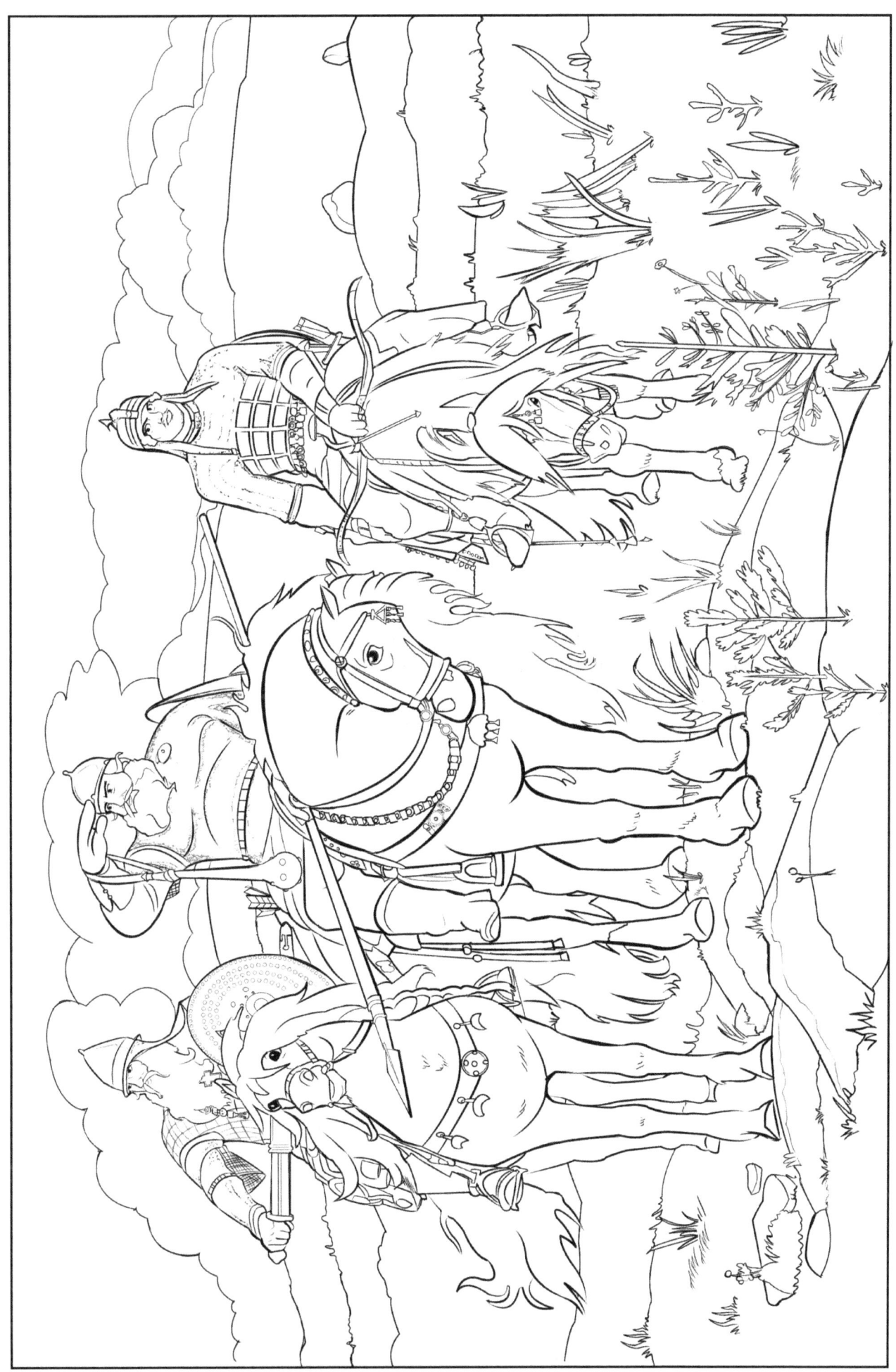

3

Plate 1. Viktor Vasnetsov (Виктор Васнецов)

Bogatyrs (Богатыри), 1898

Viktor Vasnetsov was a Russian painter, draftsman and graphic artist. He is considered to be a key figure in the Russian Revivalist movement and a co-founder of the romantic nationalistic school of painting, thanks to his lively, imaginative works depicting Russian folklore. His most famous piece, "Bogatyrs", brings to life three commanding medieval Russian knights, all of whom are drawn from the stories told in the Slavic epic poems known as Bylinas. The mythical knights are seen as protectors of ancient Rus', symbolizing the heroic past and the great future of the country. Vasnetsov's work on this painting spanned almost 20 years.

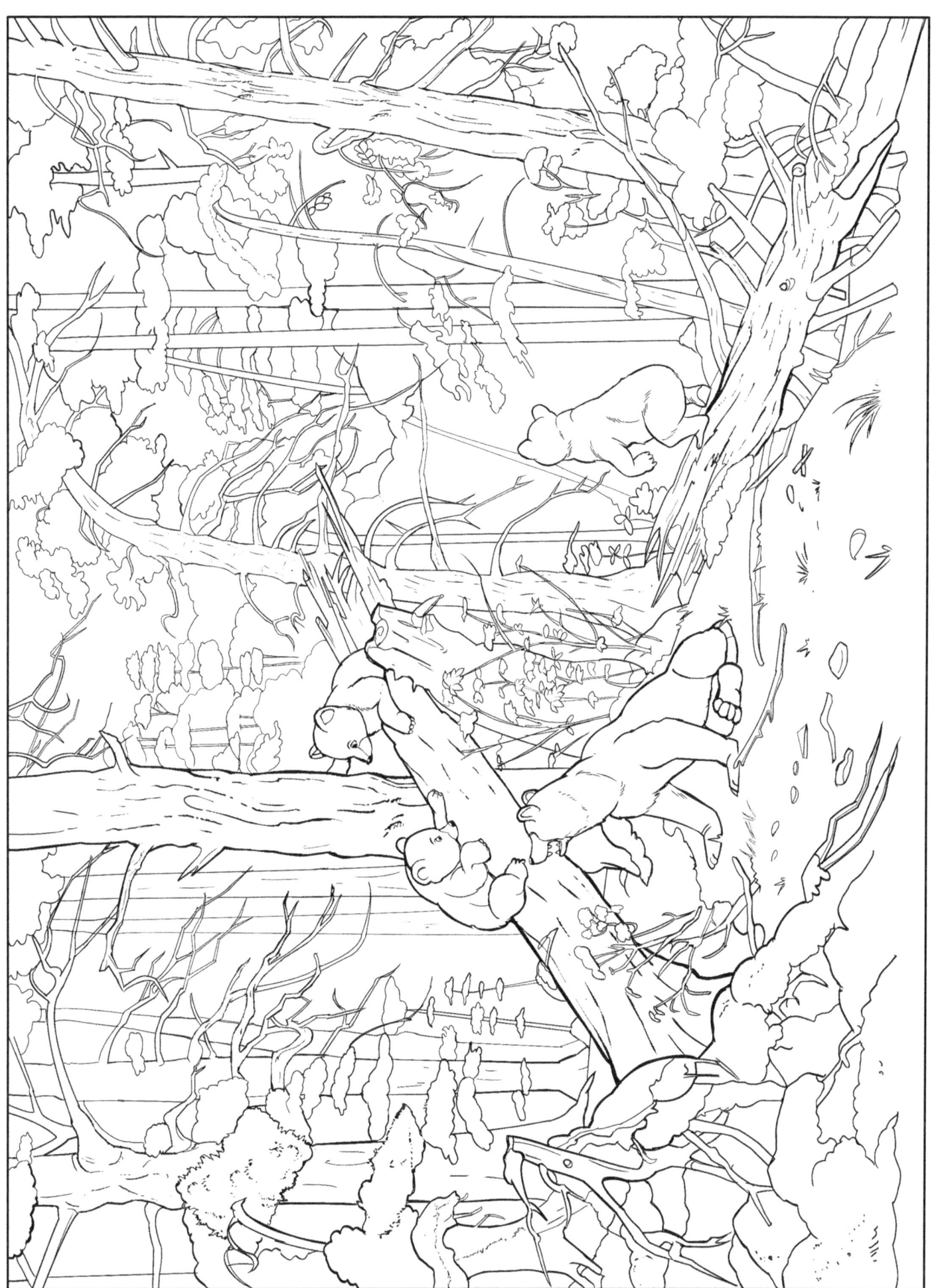

Plate 2. Ivan Shishkin, Konstantin Savitsky
(Иван Шишкин, Константин Савицкий)

Morning in a Pine Forest (Утро в сосновом лесу), 1889

Ivan Shishkin was a Russian painter of many talents who specialized in lifelike, meticulously detailed landscapes — in his case, purely Russian landscapes — as part of the Peredvizhniki movement. Peredvizhnhiki, sometimes called "The Wanderers" or "The Itinerants" in English, were a group of like-minded artists who refused to conform to academic rules and restrictions and wanted their art to be a realistic representation of contemporary life in Russia. The playful, photographic "Morning in a Pine Forest" is co-painted with Konstantin Savitsky, another Peredvizhniki member, the latter credited with the charming depiction of the mother-bear and her three cubs, who play on a broken tree trunk.

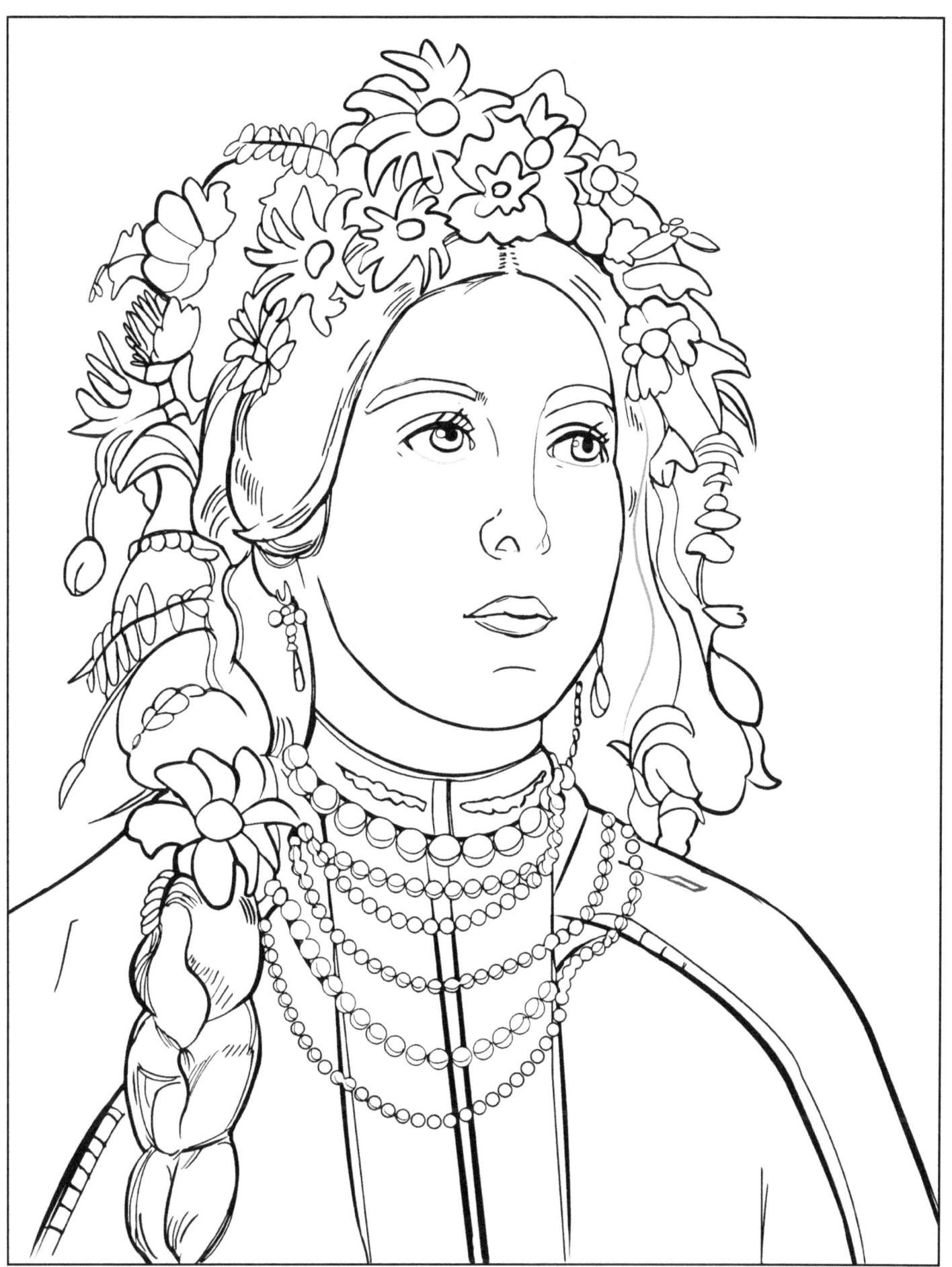

Plate 3. Konstantin Makovsky (Константин Маковский)

**Russian Beauty in Summer Garland (Русская красавица),
second half of the 19th century**

Konstantin Makovsky was a Russian painter, active during the 19th century, and a fellow member of the Peredvizhniki movement. Whereas many artists remain unknown during their lifetimes, Makovsky was in fact one of the most highly appreciated and highly paid artists of his time. Unlike some of his contemporaries, who focused on landscape, he produced stunning portraits. It is Makovsky's portraits of female sitters that comprise the most striking part of the artist's legacy. One of the finest examples is "Russian Beauty in Summer Garland," where even the brilliance of the blossoming flowers cannot compete with the bright loveliness of the sitter's eyes.

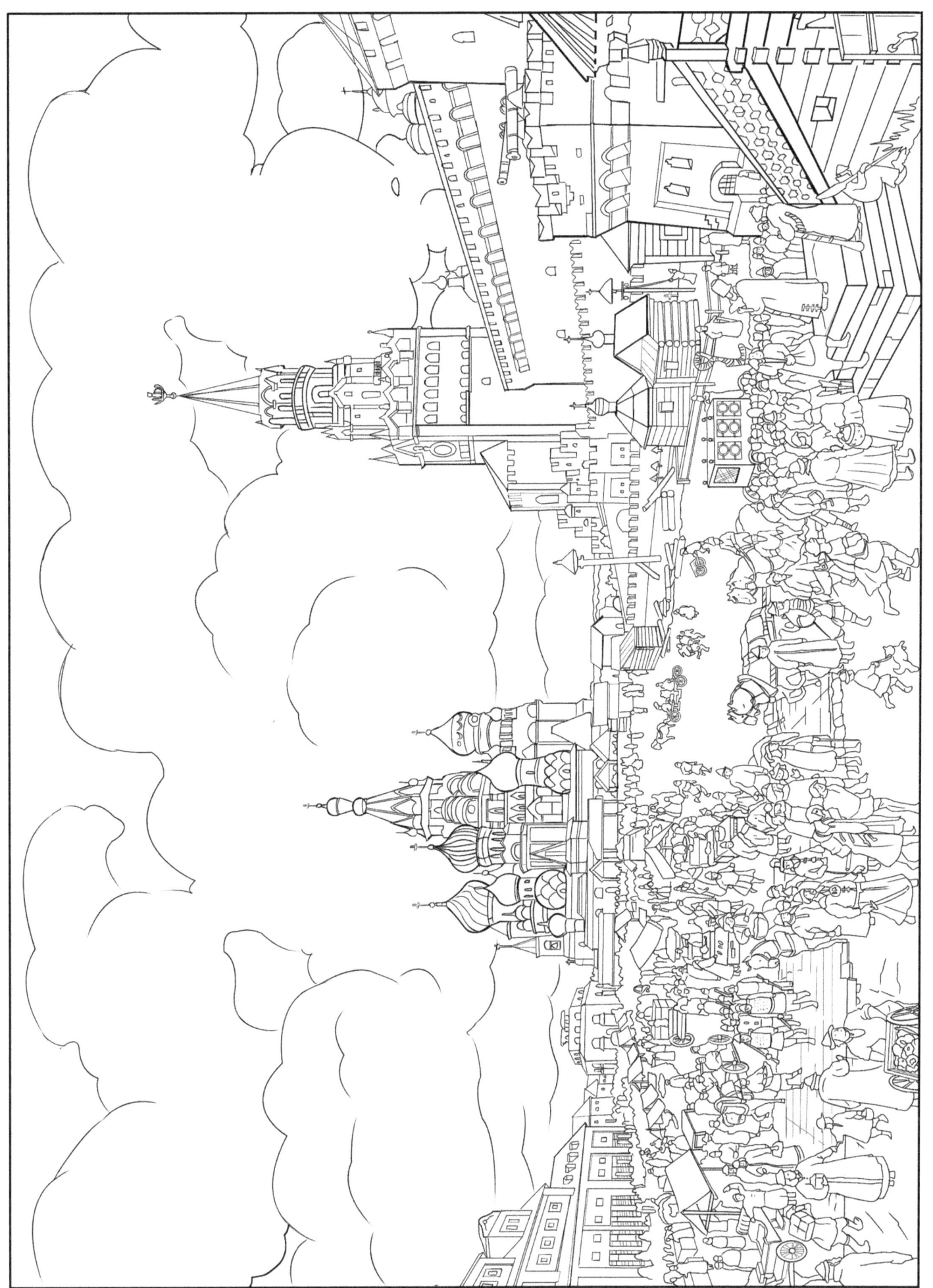

9

Plate 4. Apollinary Vasnetsov (Аполлинарий Васнецов)

Red Square in the Second Half of XVII Century
(Красная площадь во второй половине XVII века), 1925

Apollinary Vasnetsov may be less known than his famous elder brother, Viktor Vasnetsov, yet he contributed exceptional works to the artistic canon of Russia's painting scene of the 19th century. He created epic landscapes of Russian nature and was equally masterful in interpreting historical and archaeological data. His painting "Red Square in the Second Half of XVII Century" demonstrates outstanding artistic skills and is indicative of Vasnetsov's interest in depicting Moscow cityscapes, particularly from the medieval period.

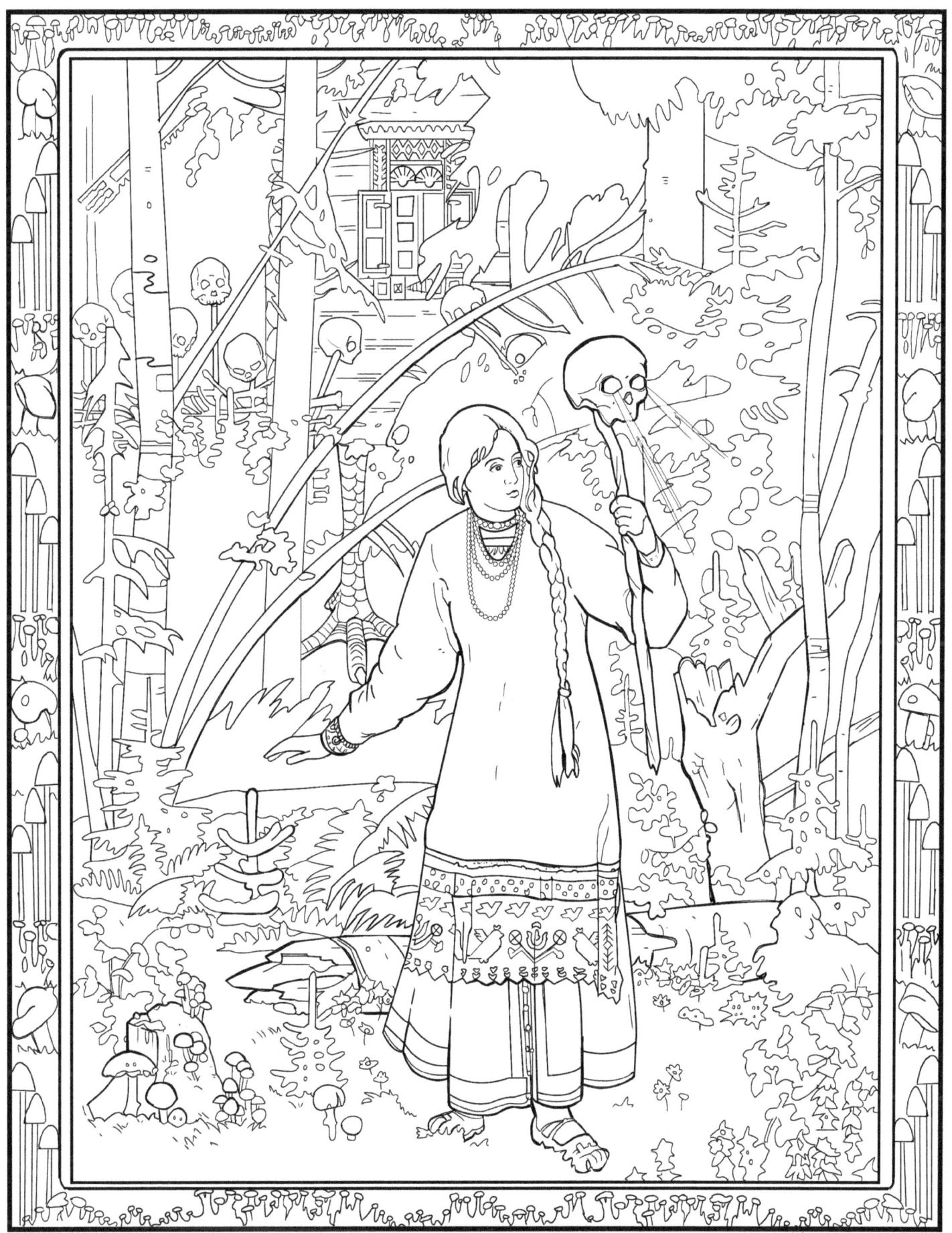

Plate 5. Ivan Bilibin (Иван Билибин)

Vasilisa the Beautiful at the Hut of Baba Yaga
(Василиса Прекрасная уходит из дома Бабы Яги), 1899

Ivan Bilibin was a renowned Russian illustrator and stage designer. Bilibin made a name for himself on the Russian art scene in the late 19th century when he was only in his early twenties. At the beginning of his career he travelled in the Russian north, becoming fascinated with traditional wooden architecture and Slavic folklore. He created a series of illustrations of Russian fairy tales, among them "Vasilisa the Beautiful," the story of a young woman living with a cruel stepmother. The stepmother sends her to the hut of an old and ferocious-looking witch named Baba Yaga but Vasilisa is eventually saved by her late mother's eternal love.

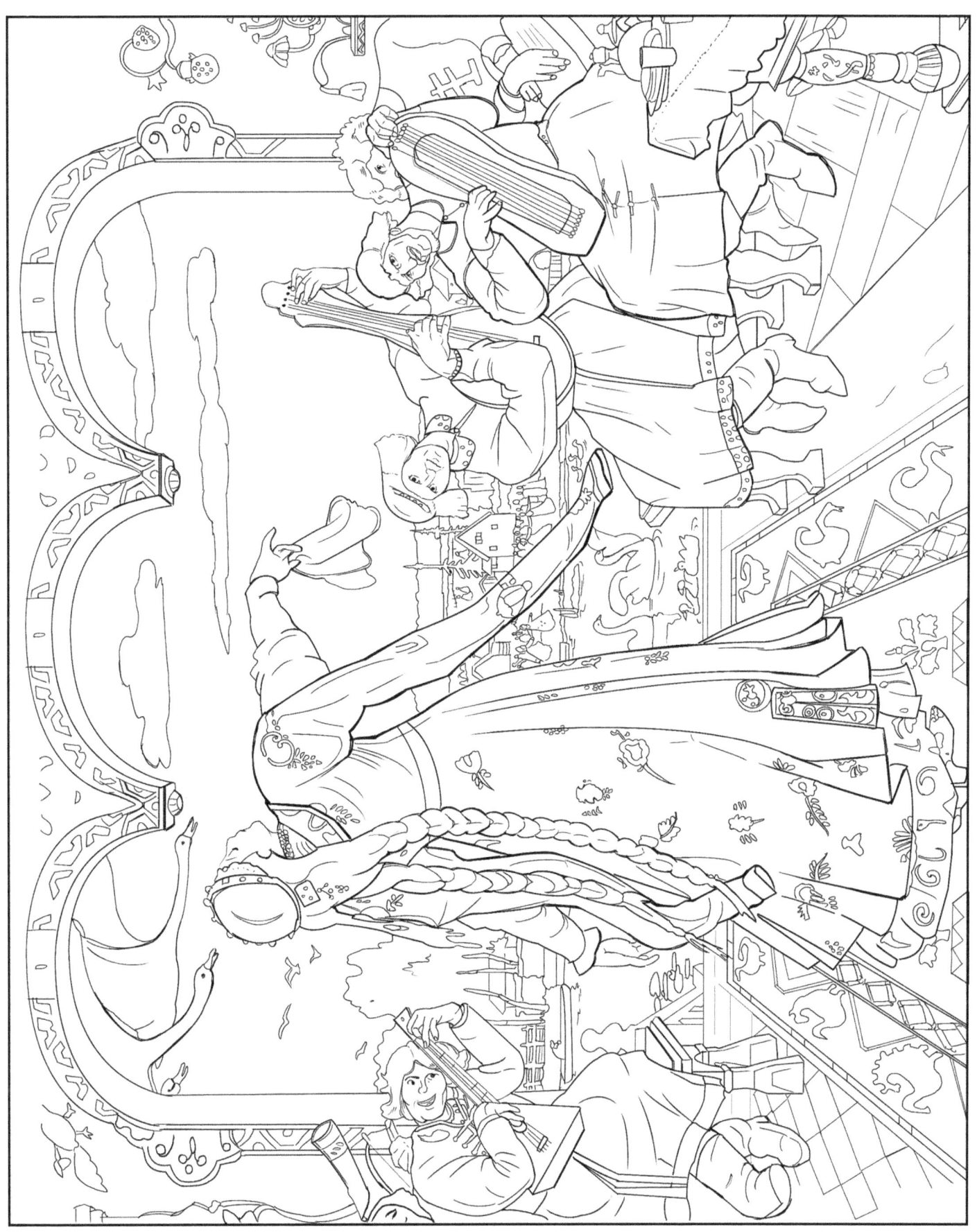

Plate 6. Viktor Vasnetsov (Виктор Васнецов)

The Frog Tsarevna (Царевна-лягушка), 1918

Viktor Vasnetsov immersed himself in art from the age of 10, when he studied at a seminary in Vyatka, also whilst working for a local icon shop and helping to paint frescoes. Later he became part of the Peredvizhniki movement and was invited to join them in Paris where he embraced the genre for which he would become most famous: fairy-tale and folklore subjects such as The Frog Tsarevna, a Russian folktale about Vasilisa the Wise, an enchanted princess who was turned into a frog and later saved by a prince. Vasnetsov's painting is a sumptuous depiction of the titular character in a graceful and elegant dance.

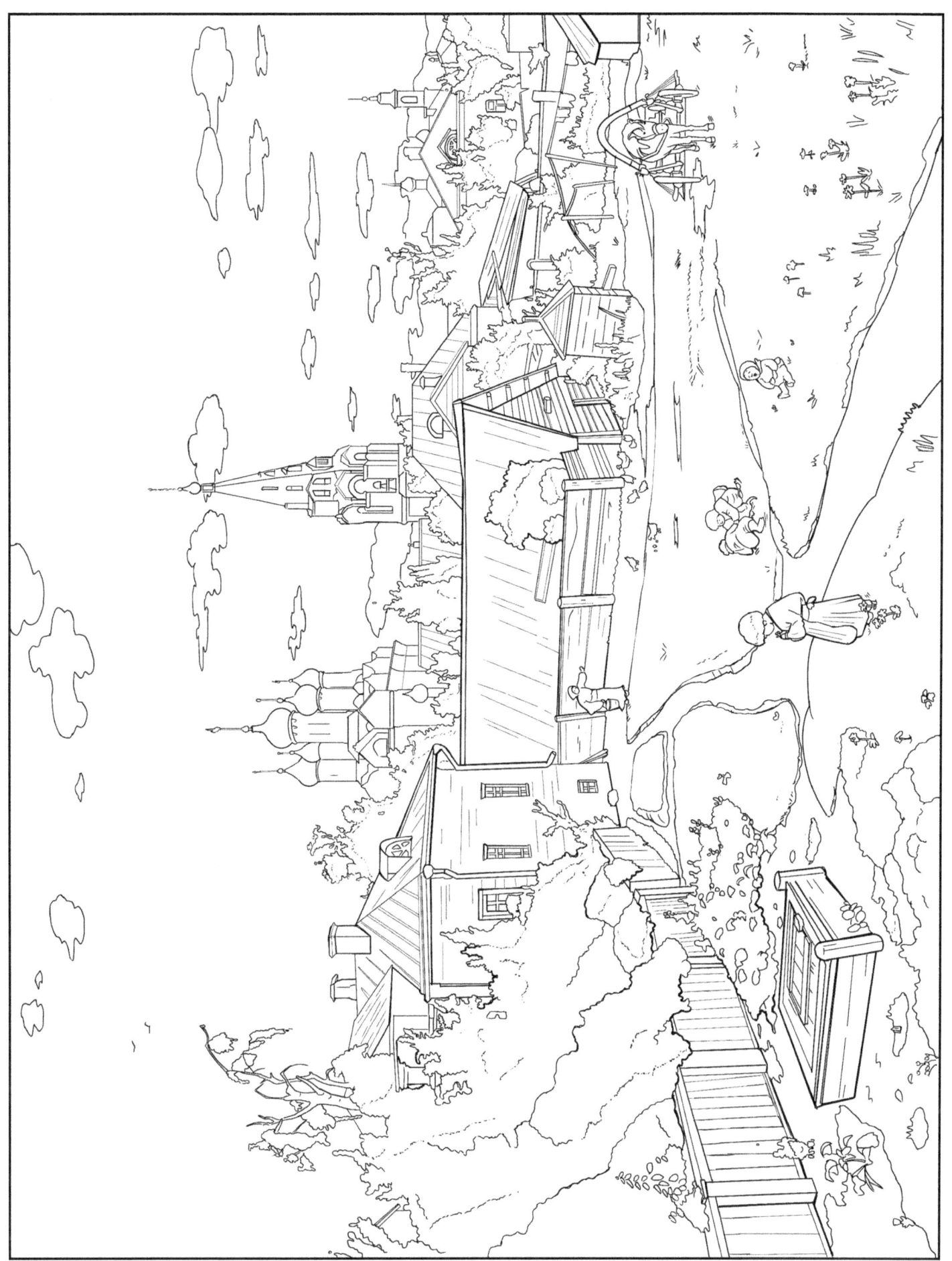

Plate 7. Vasily Polenov (Василий Поленов)

The Moscow Courtyard (Московский дворик), 1878

Painter, professor and a member of the famous Peredvizhniki movement, Vasily Polenov is best-known for his landscapes, but this prolific artist was also a man of letters; his correspondence provides insight into the world of the Russian art scene of the 19th century. One of his most famous works, "The Moscow Courtyard," is a coherent and powerful image of historical Moscow. It beckons viewers with its warm, glowing afternoon sunlight, depicting a peaceful, languid pace of life.

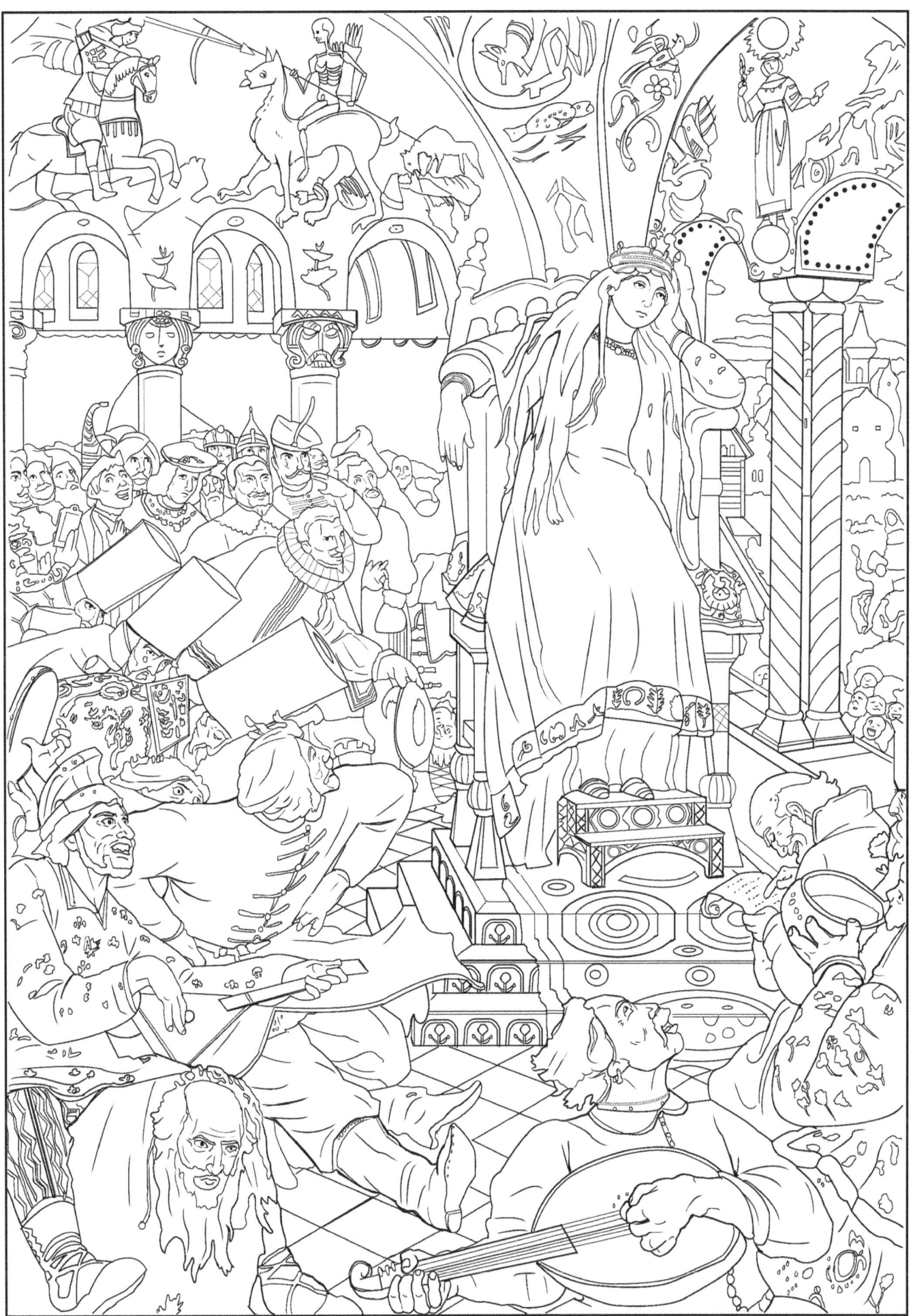

17

Plate 8. Viktor Vasnetsov (Виктор Васнецов)

The Princess Who Never Smiled (Царевна-несмеяна), 1914-1924

It wasn't until Viktor Vasnetsov lived in Paris — with the cohorts of the Peredvizhniki movement, who rejected the Imperial Academy of Arts' conservative rules and regulations — that he embraced fairy-tales as a subject choice. He produced works like "The Princess Who Never Smiled," in which gorgeously attired masses of men have assembled before the regal *tsarevna* in an attempt to make her laugh or smile for the reward of her hand in marriage and thus becoming a prince.

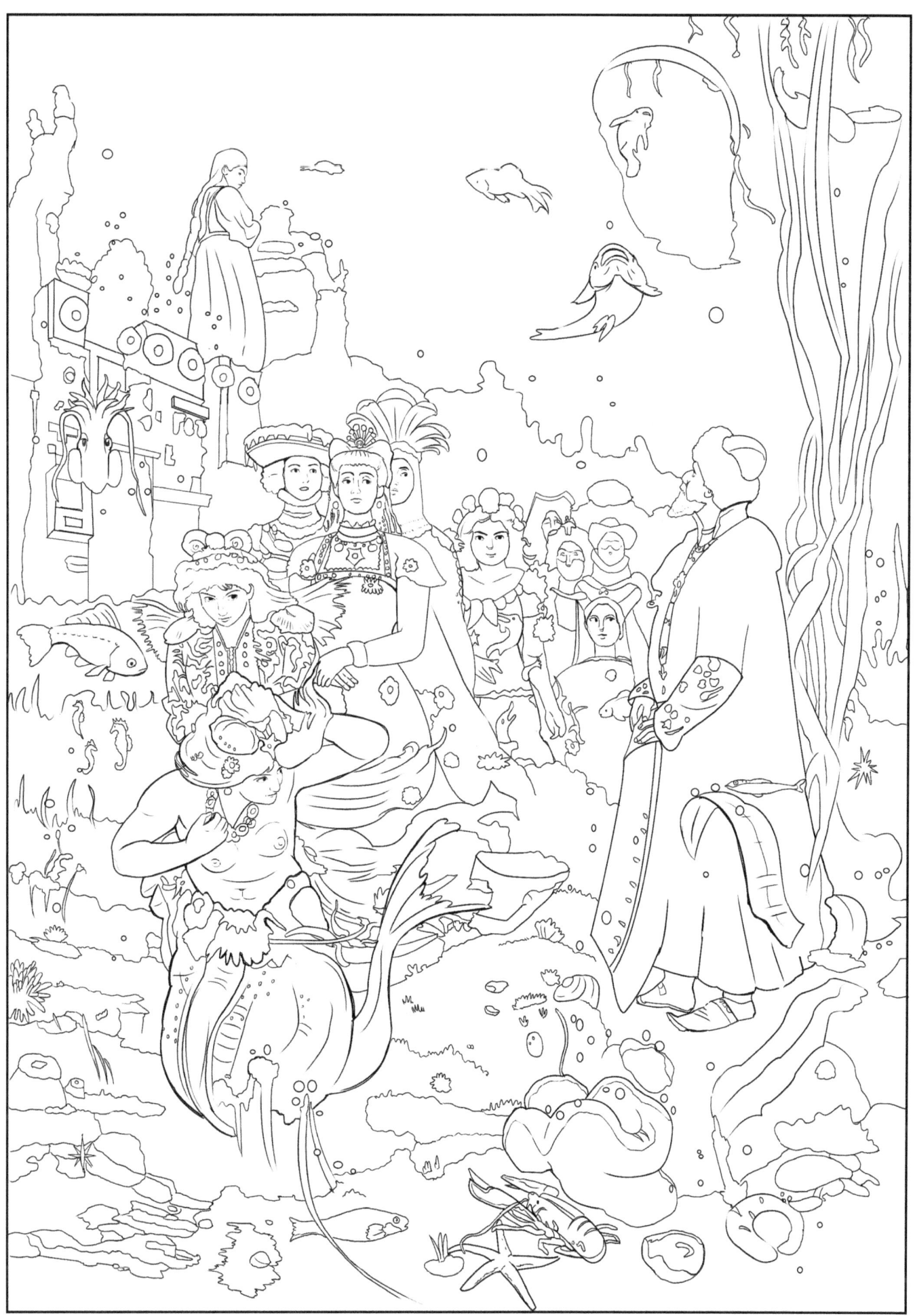

Plate 9. Ilya Repin (Илья Репин)

Sadko in the Underwater Tsardom (Садко), 1876

In Russia, the most famous writer of the 19th century was Leo Tolstoy; within the world of art his equal was Ilya Repin, an Academy-trained realist painter who became a friend of the great Tolstoy, as well as many of the other Russian artists influencing the cultural scene at the time. His eerily enchanting "Sadko in the Underwater Tsardom" brings to life an episode from the medieval epic about a merchant and a musician named Sadko. His adventures bring him underwater where he is presented with a multitude of beautiful potential brides by the Sea Tsar. This painting earned Repin the title of academician.

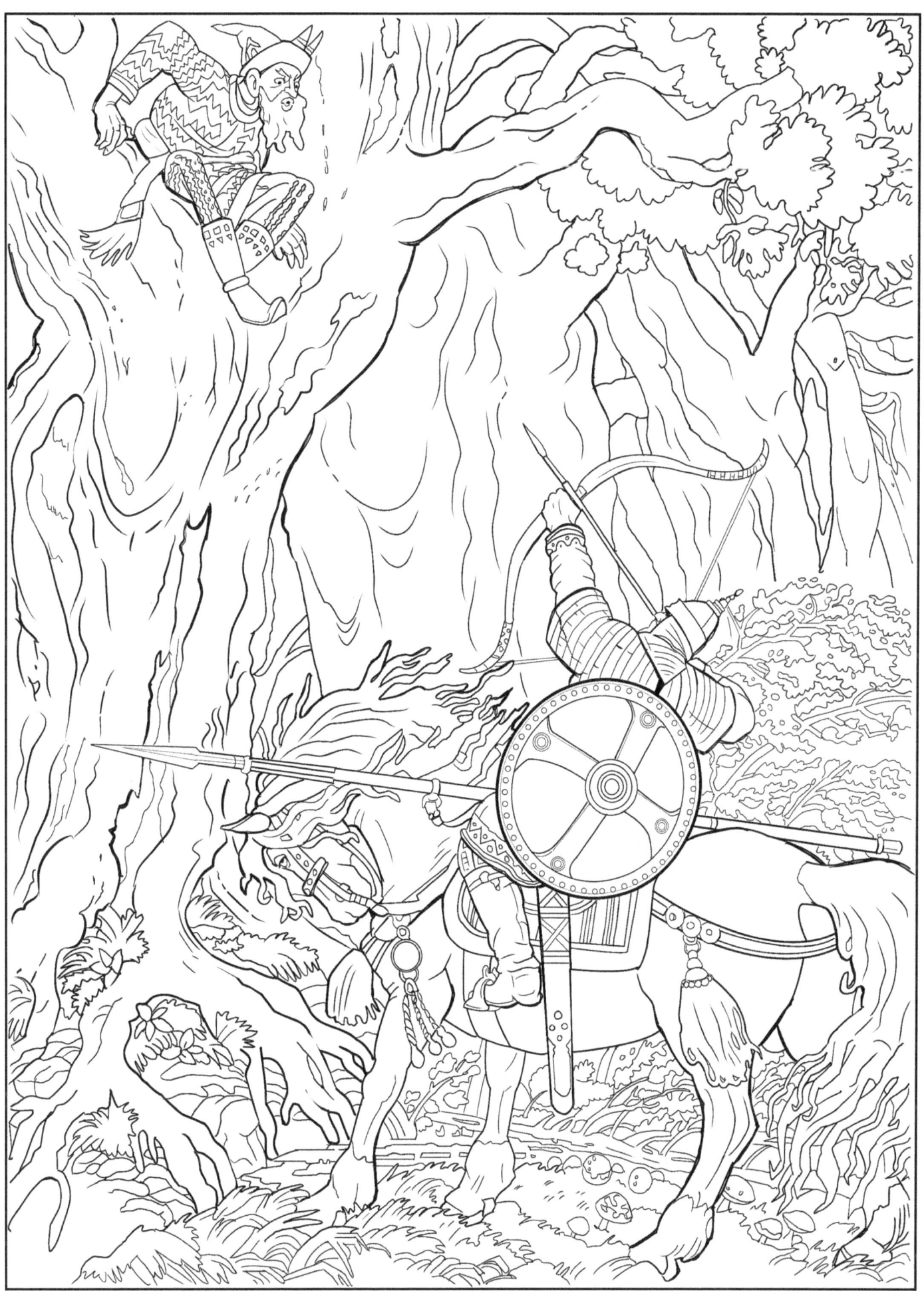

Plate 10. Ivan Bilibin (Иван Билибин)

**Ilya Muromets and Nightingale the Robber
(Илья Муромец и Соловей-разбойник), 1940**

An illustrator and set designer for the stage, Ivan Bilibin began creating illustrations based on Russian folktales in the late 19th century and continued to do so until his last years. He died during the Siege of Leningrad in 1942. Just two years before his death he completed "Ilya Muromets and Nightingale the Robber." The illustration is based on the story about the famous folk hero, Bogatyr Ilya Muromets. According to the tale, he was seriously ill and unable to walk until the age of 33 when he was miraculously healed by two pilgrims. Ilya Muromets was given extraordinary strength that allowed him to defeat numerous enemies of the country. The illustration captures the moment before the mighty Bogatyr draws his arrow and shoots the villainous monster, named Nightingale the Robber, through the head.

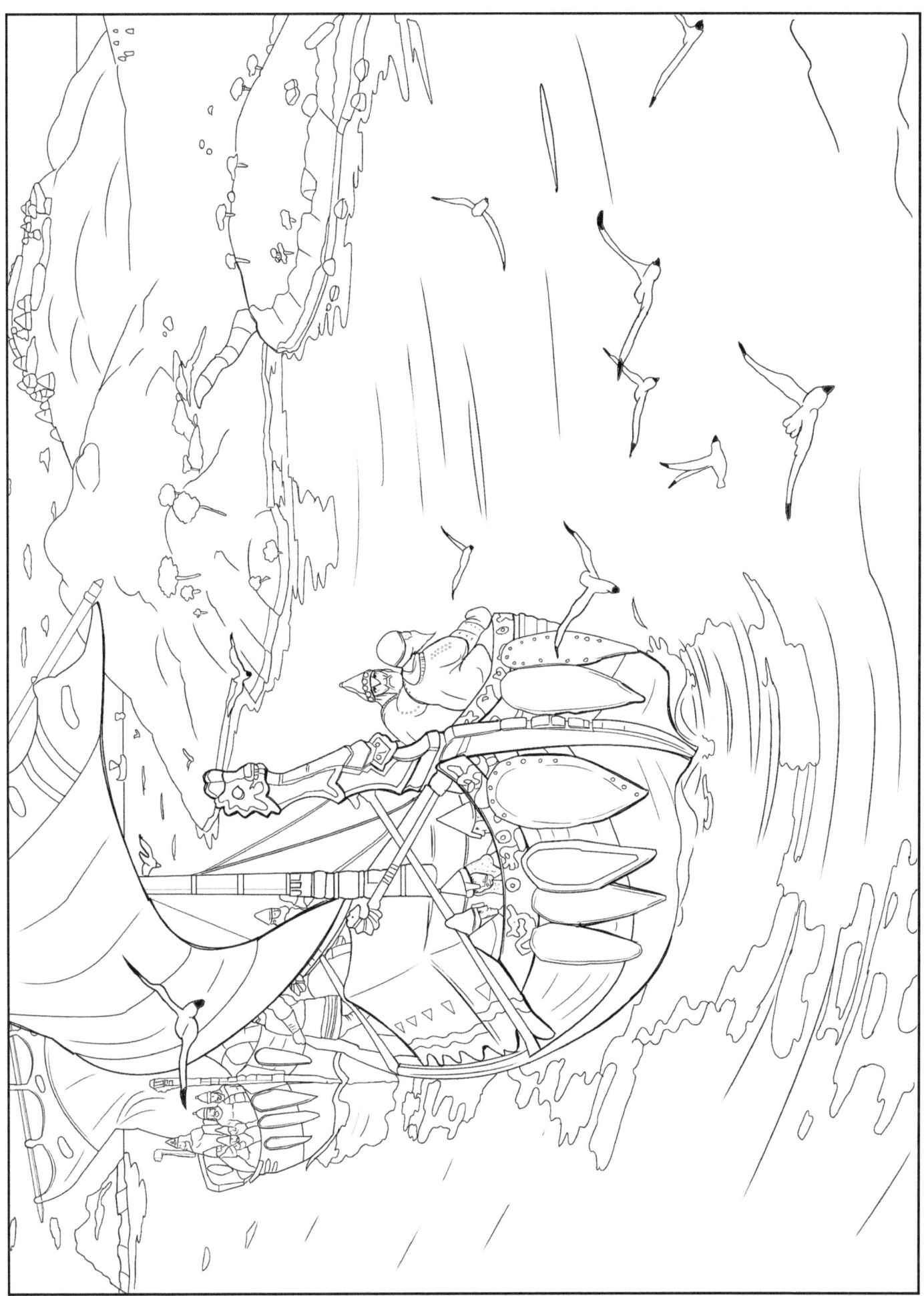

Plate 11. Nicholas Roerich (Николай Рерих)

Guests from Overseas (Заморские гости), 1901

Though he was a gifted painter, Nicholas Roerich was that and more: a lawyer, a philosopher, an archaeologist and a writer. Aside from being worldly and well-travelled, he was also nominated for the Nobel Peace Prize multiple times, but lasting legacy to the art world was in the form of his paintings, whose subjects, like that of "Guests from Overseas," was invariably focused on ancient Russian history. The painting is dedicated to the Vikings' arrival in Rus'. They are led by the legendary chieftain Rurik, the founder of the Rurik dynasty which ruled Kievan Rus' and later Grand Duchy of Moscow and Tsardom of Russia until the 17th century.

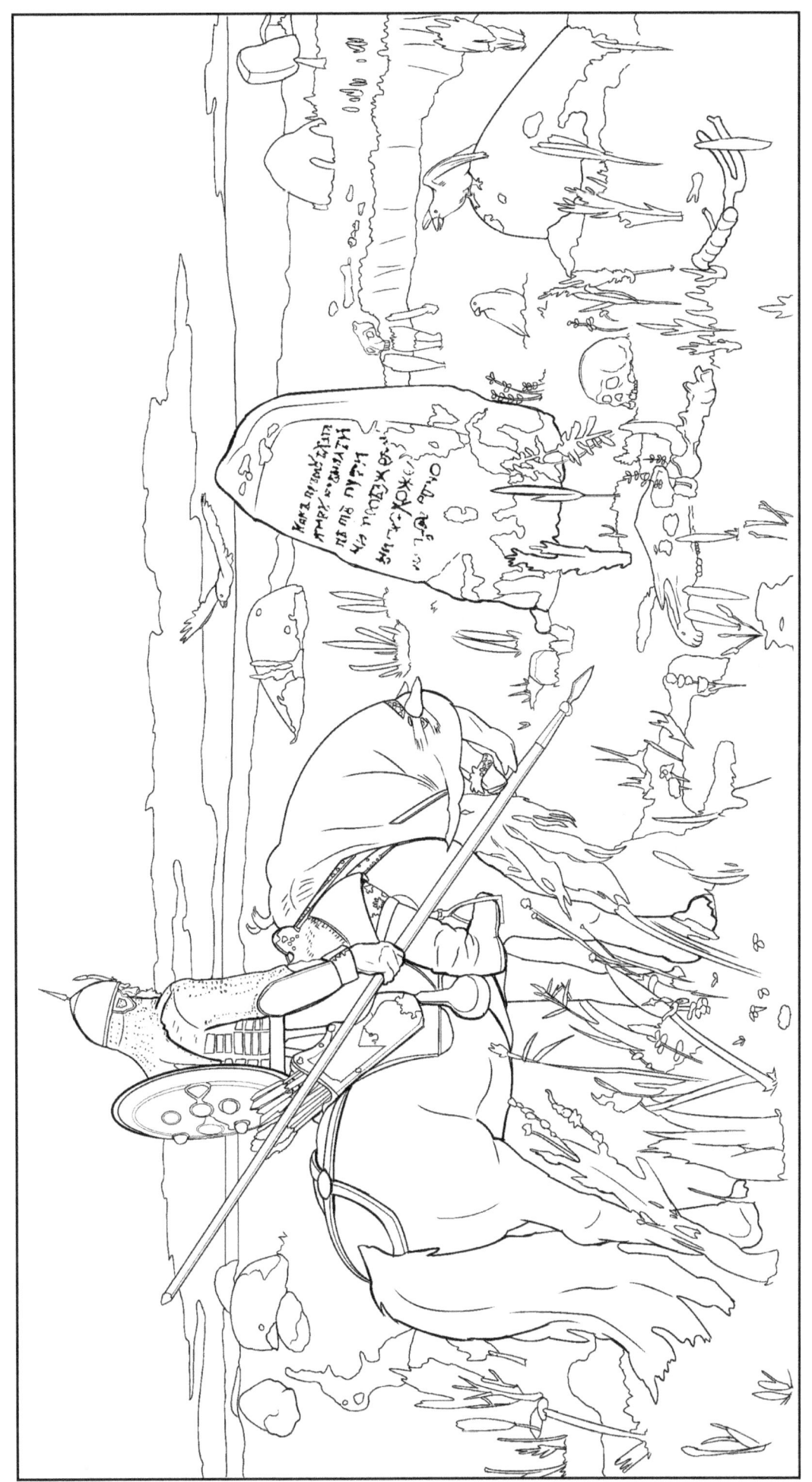

Plate 12. Viktor Vasnetsov (Виктор Васнецов)

The Knight at the Crossroads (Витязь на распутье), 1882

Few painters could conjure up the sense of what it was to be Russian more than Viktor Vasnetsov could, particularly when it came to his folklore-inspired works. Drawing from the epic poems known as *Bylinas*, his masterpiece of solemn reflection conveys a gravity as heavy as the armor and shield which the knight wears. The inscription on the stone suggests that if he goes straight ahead he will lose his life. We can't see the face of the warrior who has to choose a path.

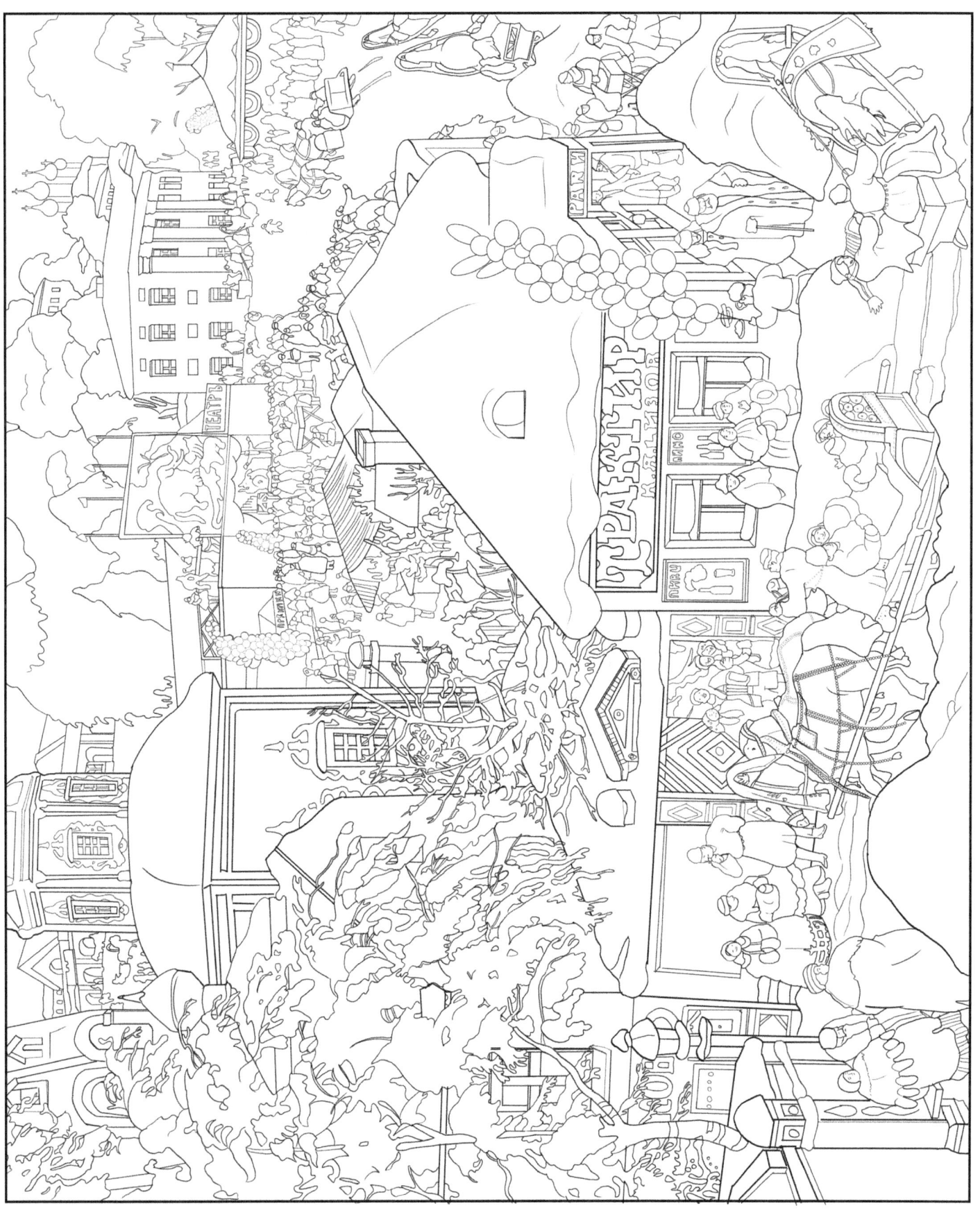

Plate 13. Boris Kustodiev (Борис Кустодиев)

Winter Festivities (Зима. Масленичное гулянье), 1919

As a young boy raised by a single mother, Boris Kustodiev's prospects might have been bleak; instead, through study and a bit of luck, he became one of the most important Russian painters of the 19th and 20th centuries, after being recognized and mentored by Ilya Repin. His love for his country is evident in the works he produced, including several vibrant paintings dedicated to *Maslenitsa*, an Eastern Slavic folk holiday also known as Butter Week, celebrated in the week before Lent, giving people the last chance to immerse in parties, music, dancing and other festivities that will be forbidden once Lent begins. "Winter Festivities" joyfully depicts everyday people on a bright day of the *Maslenitsa* week.

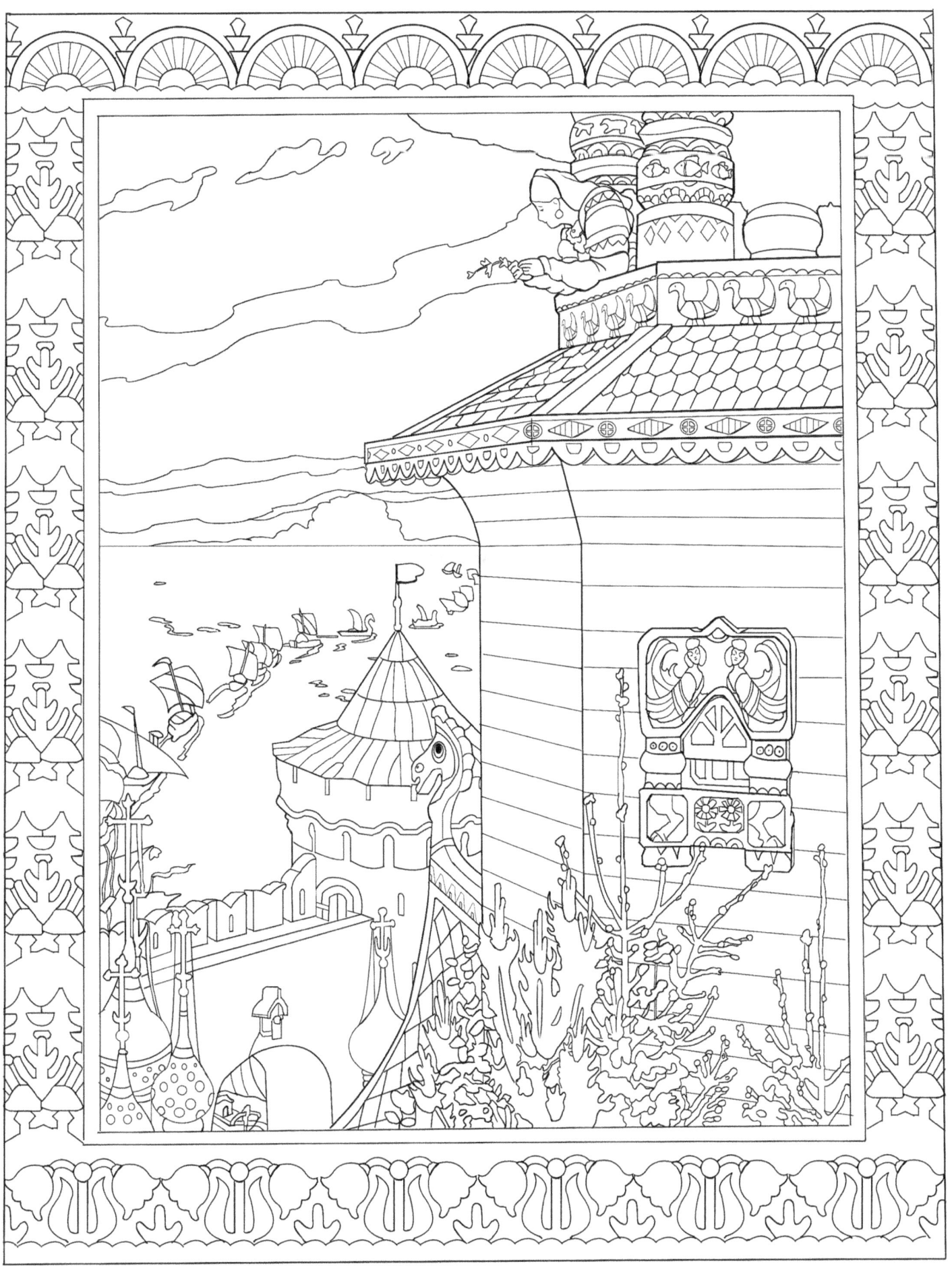

Plate 14. Ivan Bilibin (Иван Билибин)

The White Duck (Illustration to the Fairy-tale)
(Иллюстрация к сказке «Белая уточка»), 1902

Ivan Bilibin was a celebrated artist who drew inspiration from Russian traditions and folklore. While working on his illustrations to Russian fairy-tales, he developed a unique style and his own drawing technique. One of the folktales he masterfully interpreted through a series of illustrations was "The White Duck", a story of a beautiful queen turned into a white duck by an evil witch while the king was away. His best known work from the series depicts the queen gazing out at the sea from a high tower while the king's fleet is leaving the harbour. Decorative ornamentation framing the picture is typical of Bilibin's style.

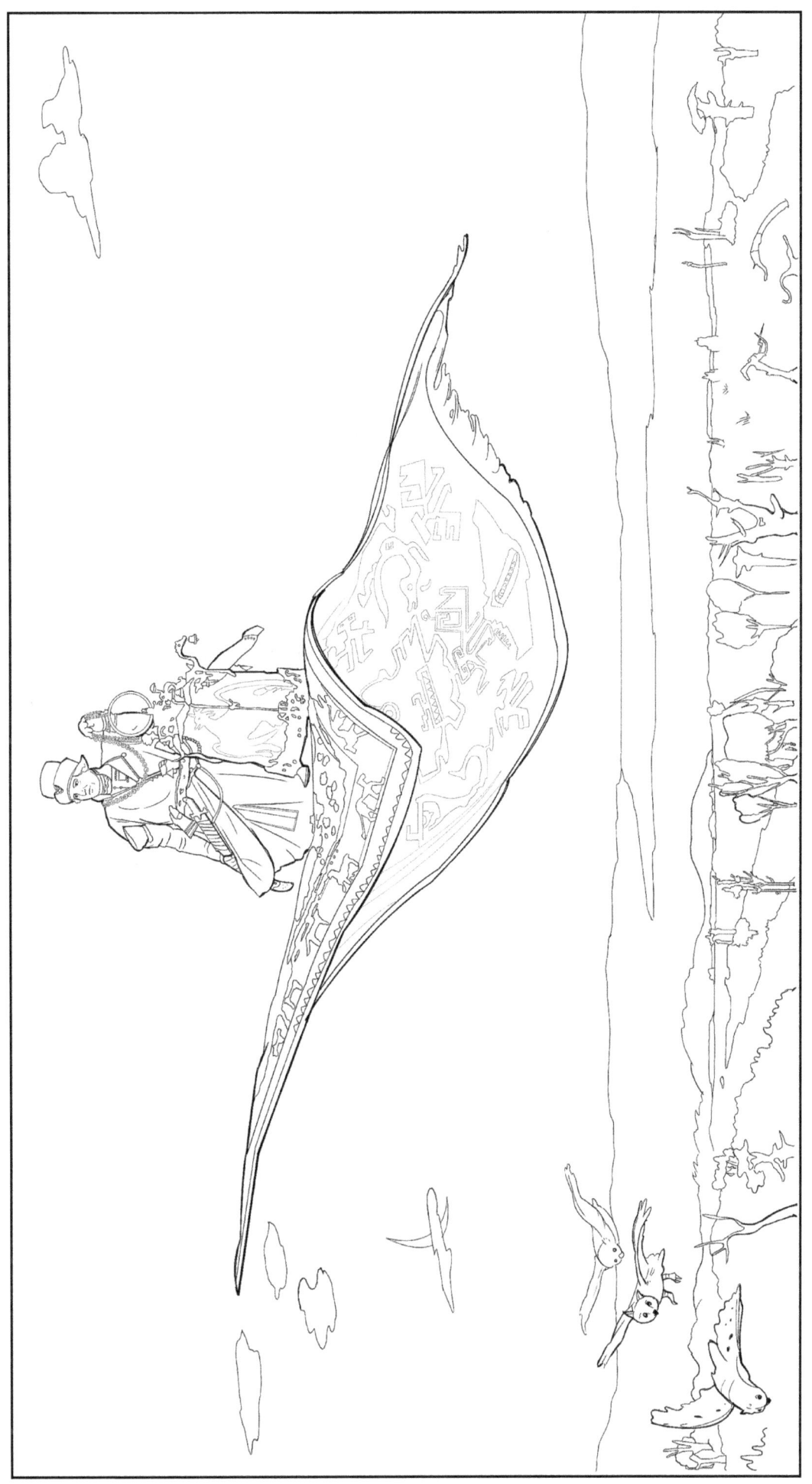

Plate 15. Viktor Vasnetsov (Виктор Васнецов)

The Flying Carpet (Ковёр-самолёт), 1880

By portraying folklore, fairytale and mythical characters so important to Russian culture and history Viktor Vasnetsov helped to define what it meant to be Russian and describe why the Russian people should be so proud of their heritage. In "The Flying Carpet" Vasnetsov portrayed Ivan Tsarevich riding on a magic carpet with a glowing Firebird in a cage, brilliantly capturing the victorious moment when the hero of Russian folklore not only caught one of the most elusive magical creatures but was also able to fly.

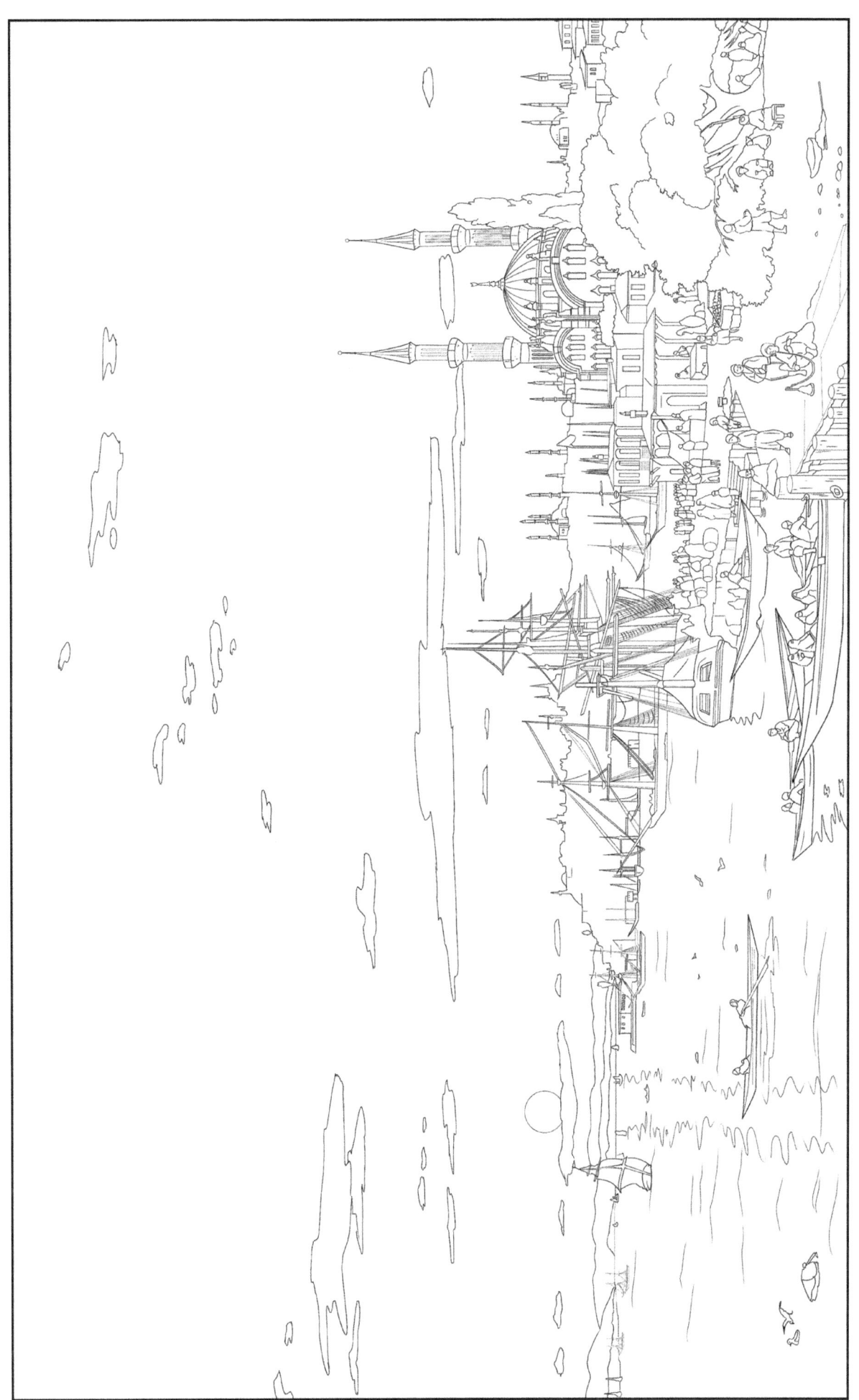

Plate 16. Ivan Aivazovsky (Иван Айвазовский)

**View of Constantinople and the Bosphorus
(Вид Константинополя и Босфорского залива), 1856**

Born in what is now the Crimea, Ivan Aivazovsky is not just one of the finest marine painters of the 19th century; he is known as one of the best in his genre of all time. His close ties with the Russian navy gave him ample opportunity to perfect a variety of sea-themed works, including the tranquil "View of Constantinople and the Bosphorus", an area Aivazovsky visited numerous times throughout his life. Created at the height of the artist's career, the painting is considered to be one of his most spectacular landscapes. Aivazovsky's work on the painting coincided with the final year of the Crimean war, but there is no reference to the conflict. Instead, Aivazovsky celebrates the lively atmosphere of a busy port in peacetime.

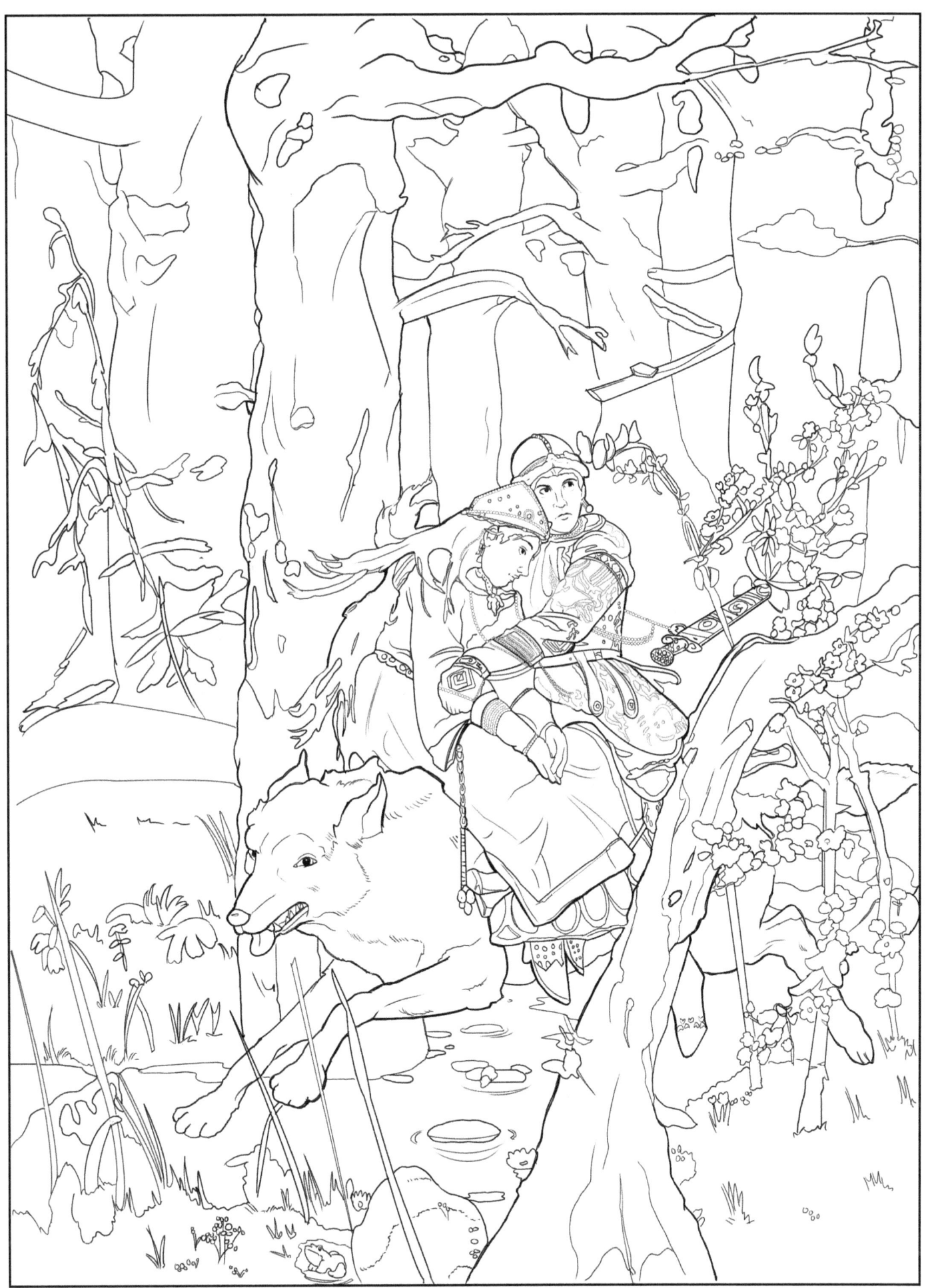

Plate 17. Viktor Vasnetsov (Виктор Васнецов)

Ivan Tsarevich Riding the Gray Wolf (Иван-Царевич на Сером Волке), 1889

In 1889 Viktor Vasnetsov was a well-regarded artist, having been commissioned to paint frescoes in Kiev. But his fascination with the fairy-tales of his homeland kept him busy on other works, including "Ivan Tsarevich Riding the Gray Wolf". This painting is not only a stunning representation of the folk hero but also of Helen the Beautiful, both of them sumptuously arrayed as they make their way through the forest. Another important figure in the painting is the Gray Wolf, a magical creature who has helped Ivan to survive and defeat his enemies on numerous occasions.

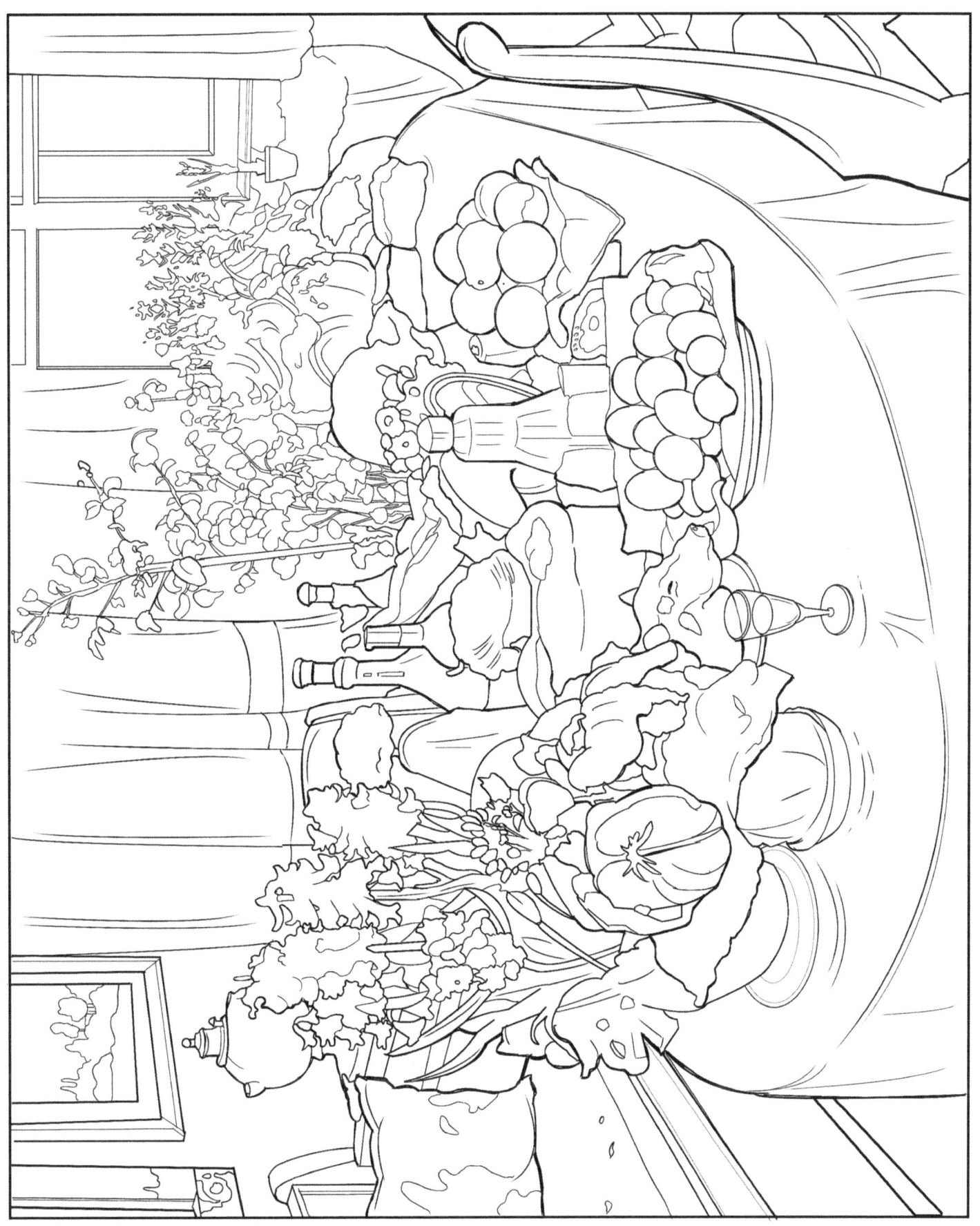

Plate 18. Alexander Makovsky (Александр Маковский)
Easter Table (Пасхальный стол), 1915-1916

Alexander Makovsky was a son of another Russian painter, Vladimir Makovsky, and a member of the Peredvizhniki movement. His rustic scenes of country life can feel as though they are in sharp contrast with his more formal works, like the portrait of the Empress Alexandra (wife of Nicholas II), but it is merely an indication of his range and his exquisite talent for conveying a variety of tones and emotions. His "Easter Table" is a colorful, warm and welcoming spread that would not look out of place at a 21st century Easter celebration.

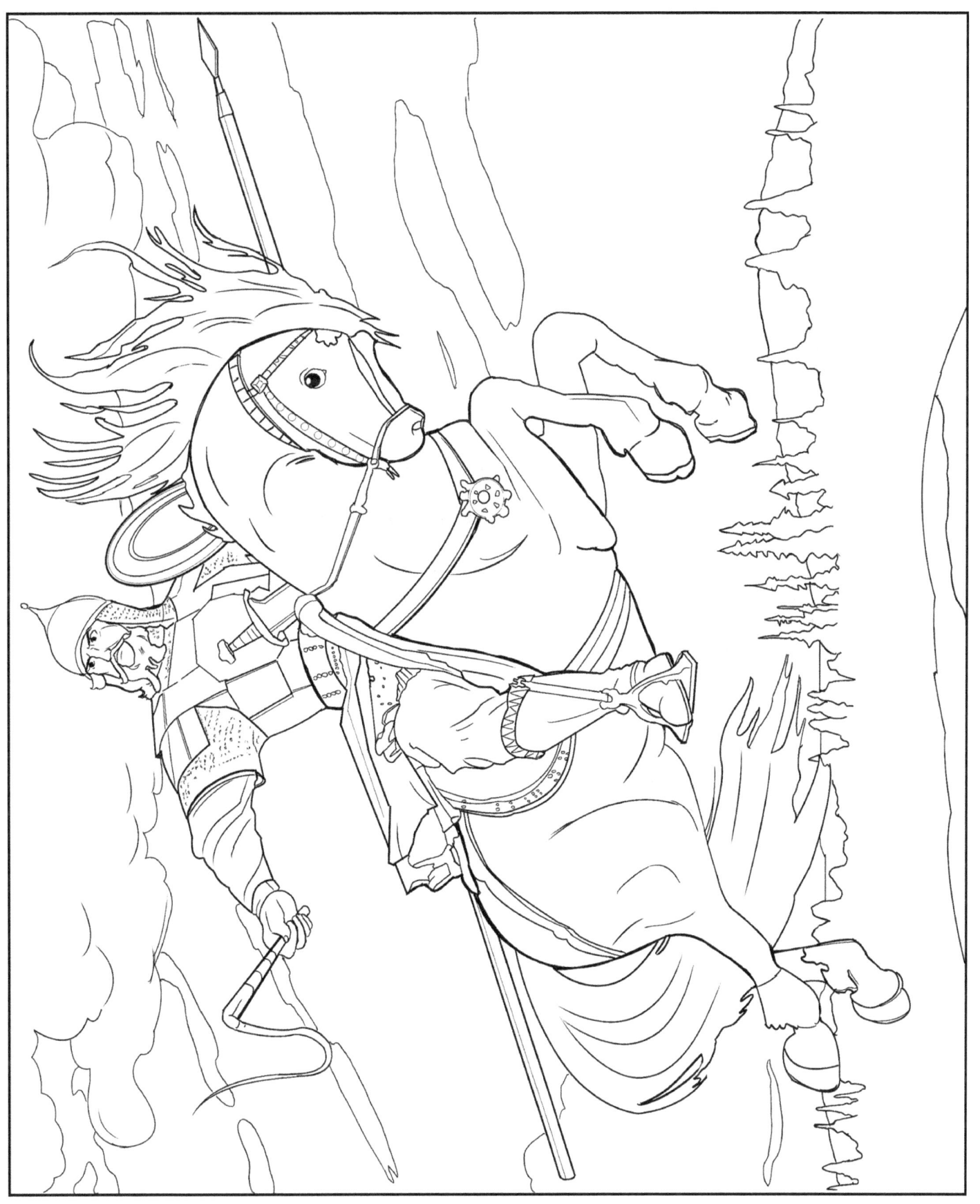

Plate 19. Viktor Vasnetsov (Виктор Васнецов)

Ilya Muromets (Богатырский скок), 1914

Viktor Vasnetsov did much throughout his lifetime to further the growing sense of Russian nationalism and pride; he achieved this by going back to the folk stories that had been around for hundreds of years. A fine example comes in the form of his "Ilya Muromets", which shows the most famous of the epic Russian knights, looking like a virile, powerful conqueror. The painting was created in 1914, when World War I had just started, during which time Vasnetsov believed that his mission was to awaken the national consciousness and patriotism.

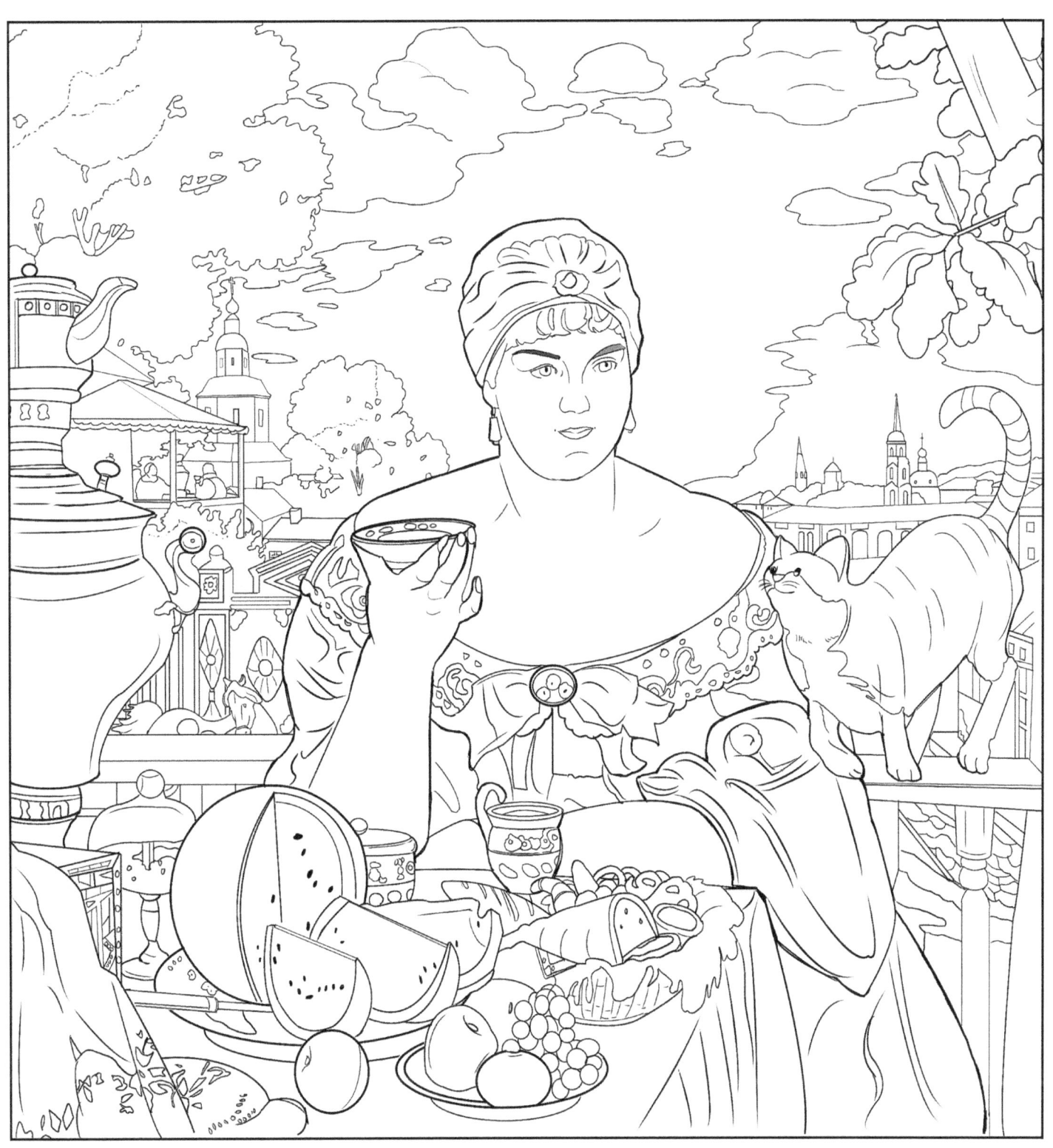

Plate 20. Boris Kustodiev (Борис Кустодиев)

The Merchant's Wife at Tea (Купчиха за чаем), 1918

With the Russian Revolution of 1917 came a new type of culture — one that rejected the previous way of life. Yet painters like Boris Kustodiev continued to portray the old ways in works like "The Merchant's Wife at Tea", where a leisurely Russian woman enjoys the fruits of her merchant husband's labours. This kind of pastime deeply contrasted with the reality of 1918, when the country was engulfed in poverty and starvation. Kustodiev dreams about simple pleasures, but at the same time he smiles at the empty-headed lifestyle, using grotesque features as emphasis.

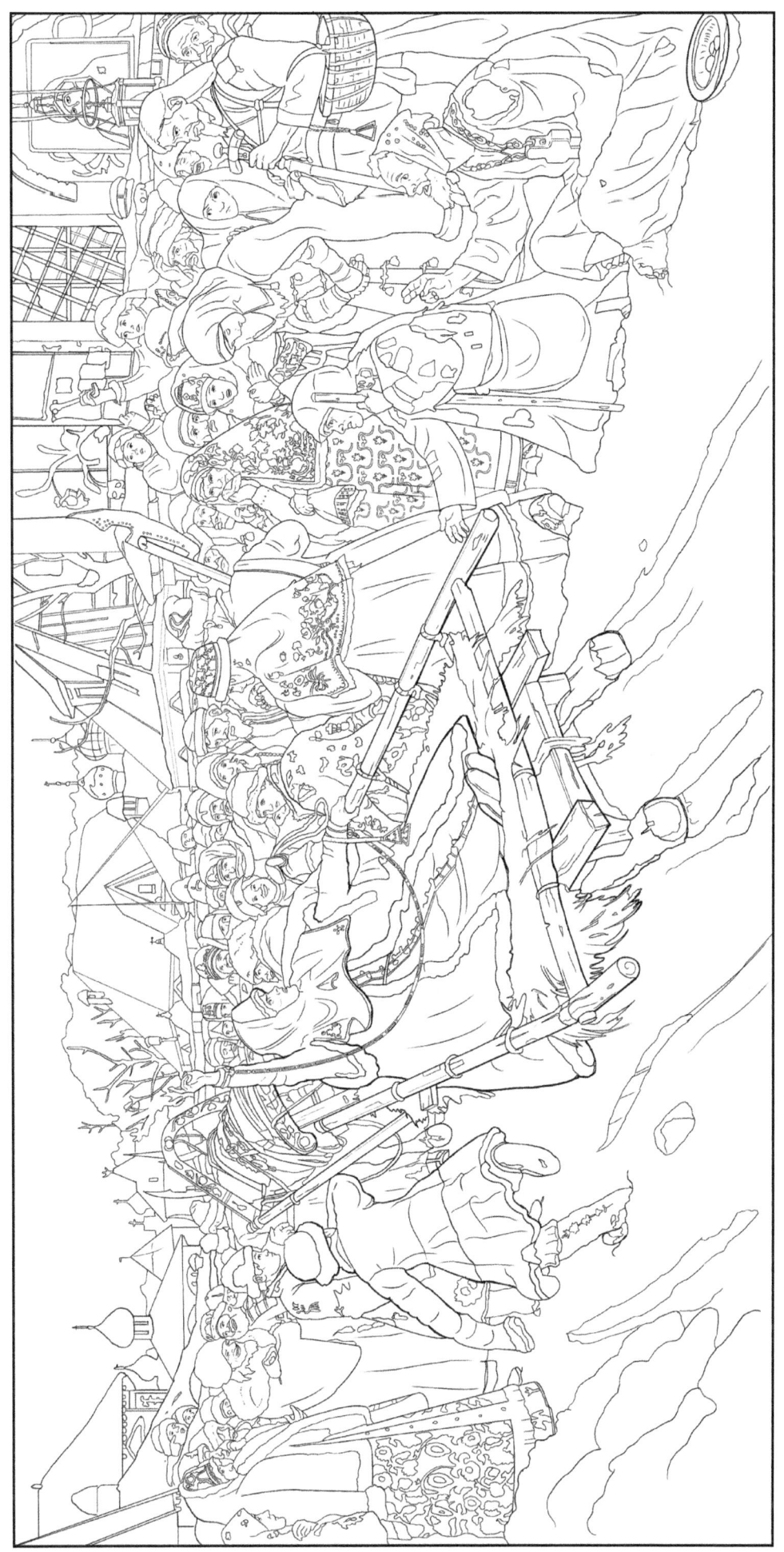

Plate 21. Vasily Surikov (Василий Суриков)

Boyaryna Morozova (Боярыня Морозова), 1887

Vasily Surikov was an acclaimed Russian artist who drew inspiration from the most dramatic episodes of Russian history. His large-scale painting "Boyaryna Morozova" takes us back to the 17th century, depicting the schism in the Russian Orthodox Church that culminated in the arrest of Feodosia Morozova who was one of the best-known participants in the Old Believer movement. The so-called Old Believers seceded from the main Church in protest against ecclesiastical reforms carried out by Patriarch Nikon and they were strongly persecuted by the state. As the painting suggests, the tragic fate of Boyaryna Morozova is met with varying responses from the crowd which has gathered to watch her get carted off to her eventual death of starvation. Being the Old Believer, she holds two fingers raised, thus showing the old way of making the Sign of the Cross on oneself instead of using three fingers as demanded by the new rules.

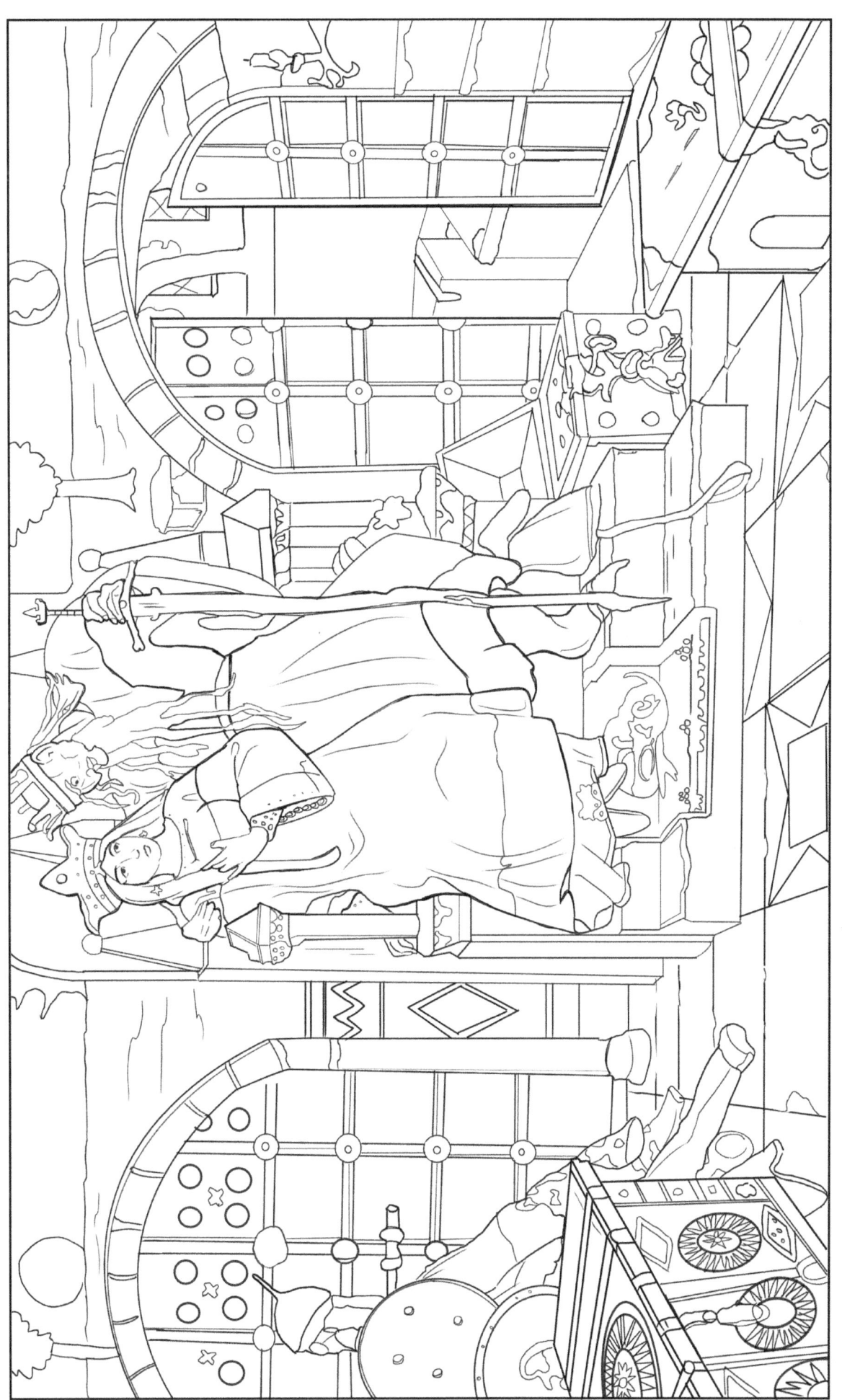

Plate 22. Viktor Vasnetsov (Виктор Васнецов)
Kashchey the Immortal (Кощей Бессмертный), 1926

Viktor Vasnetsov is best known for his romanticized depictions of Russian fairy-tales. Most of his paintings are dedicated to folk heroes and noble warriors, but "Kashchey the Immortal" depicts a mythological villain who has abducted a hero's wife. The ugly appearance of the titular character shows a striking contrast with the beautiful features of the maiden. Even though the name suggests that you can't kill Kashchey, there is still a way, according to the tales: you must destroy his soul. it is not an easy task as Kashchey's soul is separated from his body and is hidden "inside a needle, which is in an egg, which is in a duck, which is in a hare, which is in an iron chest, which is buried under a green oak tree, which is on the island of Buyan."

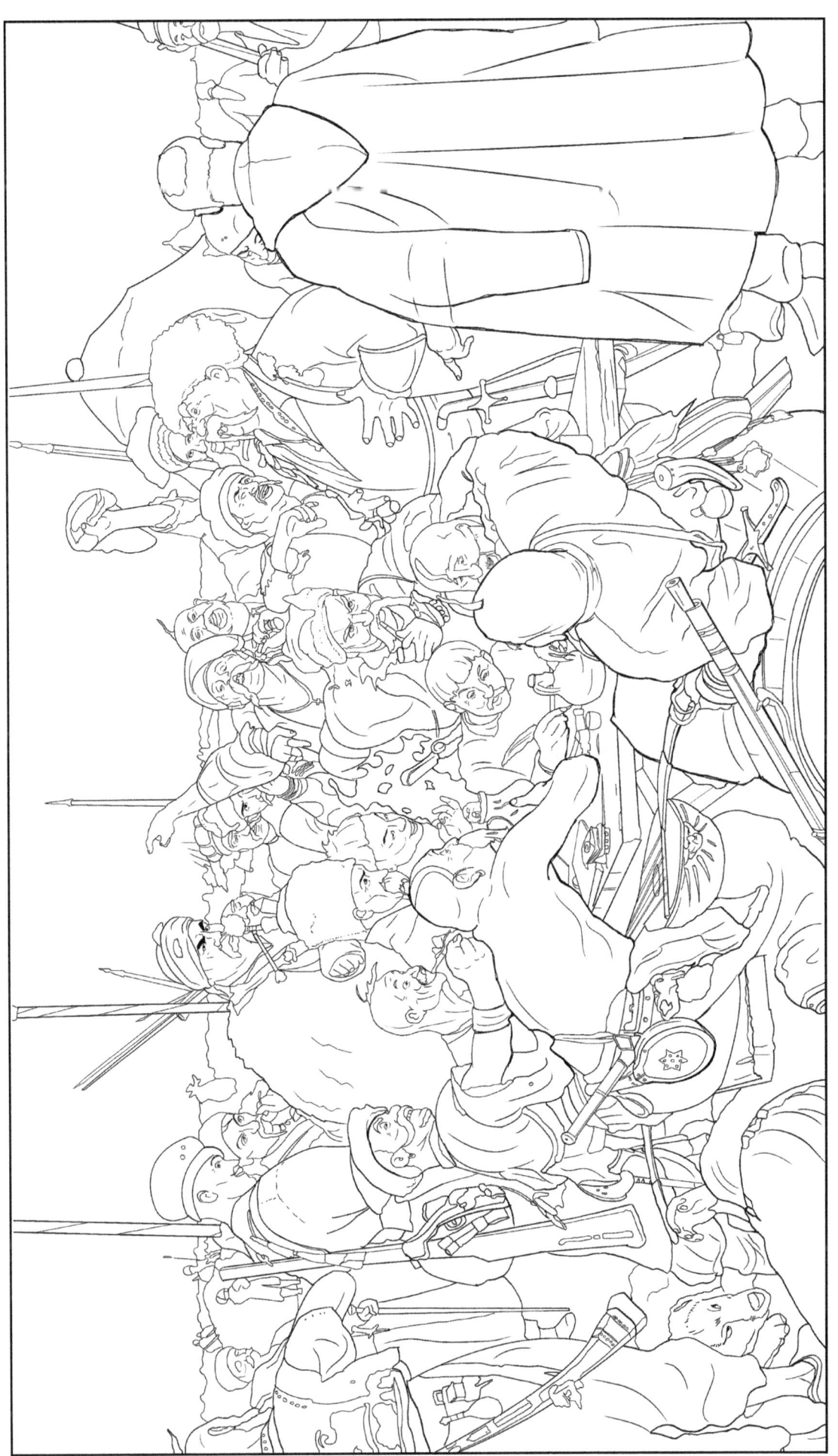

47

Plate 23. Ilya Repin (Илья Репин)

Reply of the Zaporozhian Cossacks to Sultan Mehmed IV of the Ottoman Empire (Запорожцы пишут письмо турецкому султану), 1880–1891

Thanks to his insatiable curiosity, Ilya Repin often chose to paint historical or mythical moments of great importance to the Russian people, putting great effort into pre-painting research. "Reply of the Zaporozhian Cossacks" is one example. It's an enormous homage to the legendary bravado of the 17th century military brigade who supposedly sent a letter of unparalleled vulgarity and insult to the Ottoman commander, Sultan Mehmed, in response to his demand for surrender.